· REDISCOVERING RAILWAYS ·

SURREY

The east of the county

London Brighton & South Coast Railway.

Mitcham Junction to

Ockley & Capel

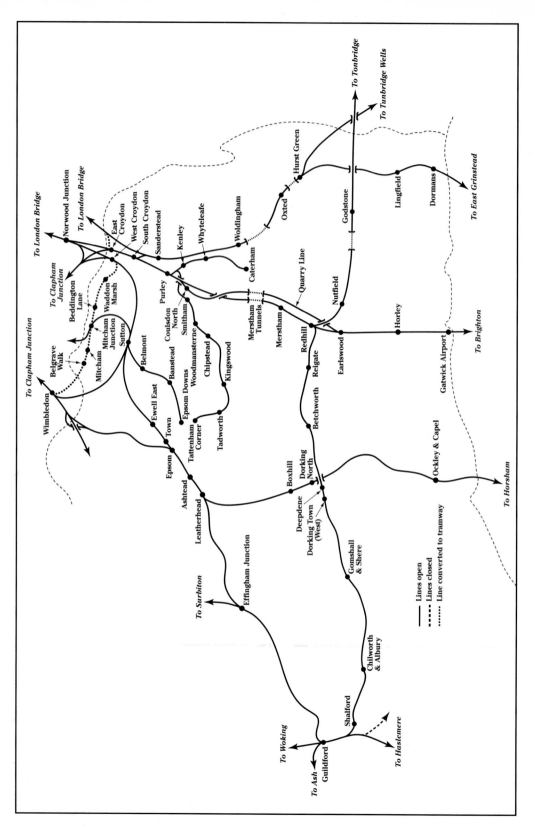

Map of the railways of east Surrey, showing the principal locations and others illustrated in the book. The railways to the north and west of Effingham Junction and west and south of Guildford are included in the companion volume dealing with the west of the county.

· REDISCOVERING RAILWAYS ·

SURREY

The east of the county

A pictorial record of the area's railways past and present

Terry Gough

· RAILWAY HERITAGE ·

from

The NOSTALGIA *Collection*

First published in 2003

British Library Cataloguing in Publication Data

A catalogue record for this book is available from the British Library.

ISBN 1 85895 215 8

Past & Present Publishing Ltd
The Trundle
Ringstead Road
Great Addington
Kettering
Northants NN14 4BW

Tel/Fax: 01536 330588
email: sales@nostalgiacollection.com
Website: www.nostalgiacollection.com

Some of the material in this book first appeared in *British Railways Past and Present, No 18 Surrey and West Sussex*, by the same author and published by Past & Present Publishing Ltd in 1993.

All tickets and other items of ephemera are from the author's collection, and all photographs are by the author unless otherwise credited.

Printed and bound in Great Britain

A Past & Present book
from
The **NOSTALGIA** *Collection*

CONTENTS

OXTED: A view at the south end of the station with Class H No 31193 on a push-pull train to Tunbridge Wells West on 14 April 1960. Normal practice for trains originating at Oxted was to depart from the bay to the right of the train.

This arrangement continues to the present time and passengers from London change here for the Uckfield line. On 5 April 2002 Class 205 No 205012 has recently arrived forming the 17.00 service from Uckfield. It is reversing and will wait in the bay for the connection from London Bridge before departing for Uckfield at 18.04.

BETCHWORTH: On 28 April 1962 the 8.20am Reading to Redhill train leaves Betchworth worked by Class S15 No 30835. Today Betchworth enjoys a passenger service with modern stock; in August 1996 Class 165 No 165001 forms the 10.34 Redhill to Reading service.

INTRODUCTION

There is great contrast within Surrey, with main lines from the London termini, the closely knit suburban lines with frequent trains, and the rural lines starting from the county's major towns. There have been many changes, some for the better, but others resulting in the railway becoming nothing more than a memory. One of the most recent changes has been the conversion of the electrified line between Wimbledon and West Croydon into a tramway.

Almost everywhere that stations are still open, the local goods yard has become the station car park. What was once simply referred to as the Southern Region now has the train operating companies of Connex, Gatwick Express, South Central, South West Trains, Thameslink Rail, Thames Trains, Tramlink Croydon Ltd and Virgin Trains. Electrification, already extensive in the 1930s, now covers most of Surrey, and relevant to this book are the Oxted line and part of the North Downs line.

There are still station buildings almost unchanged after decades, and even on open lines stations may be in private hands as houses or offices. Others have given way to new developments and many stations have only simple 'bus shelter'-type accommodation, although a few have been replaced by more pretentious buildings serving the same purpose. Station furniture and fittings have changed, often more than once during the last 40 years.

There have also been changes in motive power and rolling-stock. The early BR diesel multiple units (DMUs) still survive on the Oxted line to Uckfield, but their days are drawing to a close. All Southern Railway (SR)-built electric units have been replaced, but there is still some variety, including dual-voltage units and even trams.

The encroachment of nature is felt less on the suburban lines, but still has an effect, and some places are no longer accessible or recognisable. The policy of not clearing embankments and cuttings of vegetation has in general made locations less attractive than in the past and certainly more difficult to photograph. Against this there are a few places that are remarkable by virtue of seeing almost no changes in their appearance, where the photographs can only be dated by the motive power. The story is the same at some of the closed stations, while at others the sites are difficult to identify as they have become housing or factory estates. In some instances the only landmarks to identify a location have been distant trees or pylons, so great has been the change to the foreground.

Preparing this book has been a most enjoyable and interesting experience. Revisiting each place up to 40 years later has brought back memories of the first visit and I have sometimes been able to recall a surprising amount of detail relating to the first occasion. Some change has also been seen since the 'present' set of photographs were taken for *British Railways Past and Present No 18* in 1992.

Railway photography can be frustrating, as when watching a predominantly clear sky cloud over as the long-awaited train comes into view, or carefully planning to visit several locations in succession, only to have the sequence ruined by the late running of one of the trains. The other constraint, unique to books with a 'past and present' theme, is the requirement to take both photographs from exactly the same position. Fortunately for this book, this has been possible at almost all locations, despite the intrusion of man and nature in the intervening period.

I have taken the county boundary as it was at the time of the 'past' photographs for both of these volumes on Surrey's railways, and this book covers mainly the Central and Eastern Sections of the Southern Railway within the county. At the London boundary I have not included stations within the traditional London postal area.

Terry Gough
Sherborne, Dorset

ACKNOWLEDGEMENTS

The facilities afforded me by British Rail, the owners of private properties and others for granting me access to undertake photography is much appreciated. Several photographers have willingly provided material to fill the gaps in my own coverage of the county, and Lawrence Golden is thanked for providing the colour photographs. As always I am indebted to my wife Cynthia for her support.

BIBLIOGRAPHY

The Banstead & Epsom Downs Railway, J. R. W. Kirkby (Oakwood Press, 1983)
London Suburban, Frank Hornby (Silver Link, 1995)
The Oxted Line, R. W. Kidner (Oakwood Press, 1981)
The Railways of Southern England (3 volumes), Edwin Course (Batsford, 1973/74/76)
The Reading to Tonbridge Line, R. W. Kidner (Oakwood Press, 1978)
Rediscovering Railways: Surrey, The west of the county, Terry Gough (Past & Present, 2002)
Southern Railway Reflections: Branch Lines Recalled, Terry Gough (Silver Link, 1999)
Southern Railway Reflections: Surrey & Berkshire, Terry Gough (Silver Link, 1999)
A Southern Region Chronology & Record, R. H. Clarke (Oakwood Press, 1964 and 1975)
The Tattenham Corner Branch, N. Owen (Oakwood Press, 1978)

WEST CROYDON
TOWARDS WIMBLEDON

WEST CROYDON (1): A special working behind Class 2MT No 78038 of Willesden shed leaves West Croydon on 5 July 1964. Wimbledon trains had a separate bay at West Croydon, occupied on this occasion by Class 2-EPB No 5787, one of 15 units constructed at Eastleigh for the North Eastern Region in 1954, and transferred to the Southern Region in 1963.
    Following closure of the line from Wimbledon and its subsequent conversion to a tramway, the bay platform is no longer used. On 10 September 1999 Class 455 No 5735 leaves West Croydon forming the 13.24 service to Guildford.

WEST CROYDON (2): Class C2X No 32521 of Norwood Junction shed heads a freight train bound for Sutton near West Croydon on 10 July 1958. This location has since changed out of all recognition, with a new flyover taking the Croydon Tramlink to Wimbledon. At ground level the course of the old railway line to Wimbledon is on the left, while on the right the road, once quiet, is now a bus route with attendant parking restrictions, and the skyline is dominated by a high-rise building. The 'present' photograph was taken on 10 September 1999, before the opening of the tramway to the public, and shows No 2548.

WADDON MARSH HALT (1): Dwarfed by the power station, Class 2-EPB electric unit No 5724 approaches Waddon Marsh Halt (behind the camera) with a Wimbledon to West Croydon service on 28 September 1957.

The track has been realigned and the halt replaced by a tram stop a short distance nearer to West Croydon. Tram No 2537 is under test at Waddon Marsh in September 1999.

REDISCOVERING RAILWAYS

WADDON MARSH HALT (2): Looking in the opposite direction we see the halt on a misty morning in September 1957, with Class 2-EPB No 5739 leaving for Wimbledon. The 2-EPBs had only recently replaced two-coach sets consisting of ex-LBSCR vehicles from the overhead electric era. Coal for the gas works is being delivered by Class E4X No 32477, and on the right is Class E6X No 32411.

A driver training run with tram No 2548 passes the site of the halt in September 1999 – the tram stop can be seen in the distance. The gasworks and sidings have been replaced by office and light industrial buildings, and although the cooling towers have been demolished, the gas-holders still exist.

BEDDINGTON LANE HALT: So much clutter! This is Beddington Lane Halt on 31 July 1991 and the same location eight years later. The tram is just crossing the road seen at the far end of the platform in the 'past' photograph. The track has been doubled and the area tidied.

MITCHAM JUNCTION (1) was where the West Croydon to Wimbledon line was dissected by the lines from Victoria and London Bridge to Sutton. On 31 July 1991 Class 2-EPB (416) No 6330 approaches Mitcham Junction from West Croydon.

Here also dramatic changes have taken place and the new tramlink is carried over the Sutton line, thus blocking the view of the station from this location. Tram No 2536 is bound for Croydon George Street.

SR and BR railmotor tickets

MITCHAM JUNCTION (2): No 6330 approaches Mitcham Junction again, earlier on the same day as the previous photograph. The line on the right is for London, but the junction has since been removed and the Tramlink segregated from the railway. Tram No 2542 is bound for Wandle Park on 12 October 1999.

MITCHAM: The same electric unit is seen again at Mitcham later in the day, while on 12 October 1999 trams pass the same point, now devoid of the platform. No 2543 (right) is heading for Wimbledon and No 2431 for Wandle Park.

BELGRAVE WALK: Unit No 6330 is seen yet again on an afternoon West Croydon to Wimbledon train between Mitcham and Morden Road Halt in 1991.

At the same location, seen from ground level in the autumn of 1999, there is now a tram stop called Belgrave Walk. Tram No 2542 in Amey Construction livery heads away towards Elmers End soon after having crossed the 1960s boundary between London and Surrey (behind the camera).

EPSOM DOWNS BRANCH

SUTTON station is in the 'V' of the West Croydon to Epsom line and the branch to Epsom Downs. Photographs of the branch platforms are rarely seen, and the presence of a steam train makes this even more unusual. After a short break, this special train (see also page 9) will make the climb to Epsom Downs.

There is currently an hourly service to Epsom Downs and this is the 11.25 service from Victoria on 10 September 1999, worked by Class 455 No 5843. These platforms are also used by trains from Victoria and London Bridge terminating at Sutton.

BELMONT: This turn-of-the-20th-century photograph shows a railmotor bound for Epsom Downs entering Belmont. The branch is now single-track from just beyond Sutton, and in the 20 September 1999 photograph the abandoned up platform can be seen. The train is the 16.30 service from Victoria, formed by Class 455 No 5846. *Lens of Sutton/TG*

BANSTEAD: The most interesting item at Banstead was this lower-quadrant signal with repeater arm and unusual spectacle plate on the up side, seen in 1967. The station entrance and booking hall are behind the signal on a road overbridge.

The most uninspiring present-day photograph shows that the signal and up platform have gone. The station has been vandalised, with spray paint on the board indicating direction of travel and no glass in the waiting shelter (out of sight on the remaining platform).

EPSOM DOWNS: The view from the end of the platform at Epsom Downs in 1967 gives some indication of the size of the terminus. Race traffic, once important, has dwindled to almost nothing, as Tattenham Corner is the preferred station.

The station has since been relocated a little closer to Sutton and a single platform is now deemed sufficient. On 22 August 2001 Class 455 No 5846 approaches the buffer stops forming the 17.00 service from Victoria. After a 7-minute pause, the train will return to Sutton only. The site of the signal box is just to the left of the front of the train.

REDISCOVERING RAILWAYS

EPSOM, LEATHERHEAD
AND DORKING LINE

EWELL EAST is seen here in late SR days, looking towards Sutton. The location is still immediately recognisable in the September 1999 view showing Class 455 No 5803 forming the 09.33 Victoria to Horsham service. The new fencing seems unnecessarily high. *Lens of Sutton/TG*

EPSOM TOWN station closed in 1929 when the SR opened its new facility on the site of the former LSWR station a little further west. Class U1 No 31904 shunts at Town Yard on 28 May 1962. By 1967 the yard had closed, as seen in the second view, although the signal box had yet to be demolished. Everything has now gone, and the site is occupied by houses and associated car parking. The Sutton to Epsom line is immediately beyond the garages on the extreme right.

EPSOM (1): An LSWR train from Waterloo traverses the junction with the Sutton line. The present-day station is seen from the same position on 29 September 1999. *Lens of Sutton/TG*

EPSOM (2) station was dominated by its elevated signal box and gantry at the Horsham end. The 'past' photograph was taken in the 1950s and the present-day equivalent on 22 August 2001. Class 455 No 5842 in the centre forms the 11.45 Waterloo to Dorking service, while on the right another member of the class has arrived with the 11.54 West Croydon to Guildford service. *Lens of Sutton/TG*

REDISCOVERING RAILWAYS

ASHTEAD: The exterior of Ashtead station in 1968 shows a substantial but rather drab building. Substantial or not, it was subsequently demolished and replaced by a glorified 'prefab', seen on 25 April 1992.

LEATHERHEAD: These two views of Leatherhead looking toward Dorking, taken about 40 years apart, show little change. Although the signal box has gone, the base is still evident. On 11 July 2002 Class 455 No 5742 leaves for Horsham at the rear of the 17.25 service from Victoria. *Lens of Sutton/TG*

BOXHILL & WESTHUMBLE (now plain Boxhill) is a pleasant station, seen first in the 1960s, and again on 20 October 1999 in poor light. Class 455 No 5804 works the 14.33 Waterloo to Horsham service. *Lens of Sutton/TG*

SURREY: THE EAST OF THE COUNTY

London Brighton and South Coast Railway.

Horeham Road to

Dorking

DORKING NORTH: SR 4-SUB No 4302, built in 1925, stands at the island platform at Dorking North forming a Waterloo to Horsham service in the 1950s.

A visit on 22 August 2001 found that the sidings had been removed and the station rebuilt. In the platforms are Class 455 Nos 5917 and 5843 forming the 12.45 service from Waterloo and the 12.33 from Victoria respectively. *Lens of Sutton/TG*

OCKLEY & CAPEL: My first visit to Ockley & Capel was in 1960, and another visit on 18 May 1992 found that all the station buildings were still in place. The train is Class 2-EPB No 6324 forming the 09.59 service from Horsham to Victoria. Outside peak periods there was an hourly weekday-only service between Horsham and Dorking and no trains on Sundays.

In 2002 all trains run through to Victoria, but there is still no Sunday service. The rolling-stock has changed and Class 455 No 5806 forms the 15.07 from Horsham on 4 April 2002.

BRIGHTON MAIN LINE (EAST CROYDON TO GATWICK AIRPORT)

EAST CROYDON (1): An excellent view of East Croydon is obtained from the main road overbridge north of the station. The pre-electrification view shows the extent of the station and goods yard.

   The goods yard has since been closed and the land redeveloped, but the station remains very busy. On 8 March 2002 a Gatwick Express from Victoria is in the hands of an eight-car 'Juniper' electric unit of Class 460, introduced the previous year. *Courtesy Neil Davenport/TG*

EAST CROYDON (2): This second photograph of East Croydon before electrification is looking north from the station overbridge. The station has since been extensively rebuilt, but there is still a very similar view on 4 October 1999 as the 11.12 Tattenham Corner to London Bridge service is worked by a two-coach unit of Class 456.
Lens of Sutton/TG

EAST CROYDON (3): A pre-Grouping photograph of Class B4 No 61 on an up train at East Croydon. Despite extensive electrification, today there are still three morning and two evening rush-hour services operated by DMUs, all being through trains to or from Uckfield. On 8 March 2002 the second up train, which left Uckfield at 06.56, has just arrived at East Croydon from where it will run non-stop to London Bridge. The leading unit is Class 205 No 205028 and the rear unit No 205032. *Courtesy Neil Davenport/TG*

EAST CROYDON (4): Another pre-Grouping photograph showing Class I3 No 28 approaching East Croydon on a down train.

The last of the through trains from Uckfield runs fast from East Croydon to Victoria, and on 8 March 2002 it is worked by Class 205 Nos 205025 and 205018. *Courtesy Neil Davenport/TG*

SOUTH CROYDON (1): A study of electric traction: in the top photograph SR-built Class CC No 20002 approaches South Croydon in 1957. The three locomotives of this class were regularly used on Victoria to Newhaven boat trains. The centre photograph shows the BR equivalent, Class 73 No 73208, propelling a Gatwick Airport to Victoria train on 26 April 2001. These locomotives have almost all been replaced by new multiple units of Class 460; No 460006 passes the same point on the same day. *N. C. Simmons, courtesy Hugh Davies/TG (2)*

Opposite page SOUTH CROYDON (2): An example of modern steam and pre-Grouping coaches, as Class 4MT No 80014 and an SECR 'Birdcage' set pass through South Croydon in 1957 forming a Tunbridge Wells West to London Bridge train.

On 26 April 2001 Class 60 No 60015 works an empty aggregates train from Ardingly to Whatley. *N. C. Simmons, courtesy Hugh Davies/ TG*

REDISCOVERING RAILWAYS

PURLEY: This early photograph of Purley, looking north towards East Croydon, shows the Tattenham Corner and Caterham lines on the right, the up and down local lines to Brighton in the centre, and on the far left the Brighton fast lines.

Despite electrification and other changes, including lengthening of the island platform on the left, the 2002 view is very similar. On 8 March Class 930 route-learning unit No 930082 – formerly 4CEP No 1505 reduced to three coaches – passes through the station towards Brighton. *Lens of Sutton/TG*

COULSDON NORTH was on the main line to Brighton that circumvented Redhill, known as the Quarry Line. This view is looking north; the line to Redhill and Brighton is to the right of the signal box, while on the extreme left behind the other signal box is Smitham station on the Tattenham Corner branch.

Coulsdon North has since closed, but both the Brighton lines are still in evidence. Smitham station is still open, but hidden from view by the trees and buildings. On 25 October 1999 a Virgin train, the 06.20 Preston to Brighton, hauled by Class 47 No 47845, passes the site of the station. *Lens of Sutton/TG*

MERSTHAM is seen in LBSCR days during the re-siting of the footbridge over the Brighton line. The Quarry Line is a short distance to the right, out of sight in this photograph, but visible from the station.

On 5 October 1999 Thameslink Class 319 No 319370 forms the 08.14 Brighton to Bedford, and is taking this route despite not stopping at either Redhill or Merstham. *Lens of Sutton/TG*

REDISCOVERING RAILWAYS

REDHILL station consists of an island platform used by London-bound trains and those from Guildford and Tonbridge, while the platform on the extreme right is normally used by Brighton-bound trains. On 10 April 1992 Class 101 Network Southeast DMU No L836 leaves with the 09.20 Gatwick Airport to Reading service, having reversed in the station; there is a 10-minute wait at Redhill, which is more than enough time for this manoeuvre.

Electric unit Class 508 No 508207 in Connex South Eastern livery leaves Redhill on 5 October 1999 forming the 09.17 London Bridge to Maidstone West service, still displaying its inward destination. The Class 508 EMUs were built in 1979-80 as four-car units for the Southern Region, but were transferred to Merseyside in the mid 1980s as three-car units. Some were transferred back to the South of England in 1998; this particular unit was No 508016 on the SR and 508116 on Merseyrail.

REDHILL SHED: Two 4-4-0s stand in store at the rear of the shed on 5 September 1959. Class D1 No 31247 was rebuilt from the original D Class in 1921, and Class L No 31771 was built in 1914.

   Although the locomotive shed has been demolished, the site continued to be used as a stabling point. On 10 April 1992 Class 33 No 33201 and Class 73 No 73119 *Kentish Mercury* stand in exactly the same position as the steam engines 33 years earlier.

EARLSWOOD (1): This view of the station looking north in SR days shows the up and down Brighton line via Redhill to the left and the Quarry Line to the right. Only remnants of the Quarry Line platforms now remain, and the Quarry line is fenced off from the down line from Redhill. On 5 October 1999 Class 508 No 508203 forms the 10.48 Three Bridges to Tunbridge Wells service. *Lens of Sutton/TG*

Earlswood Station.

EARLSWOOD (2): These are the Redhill lines, looking south in LBSCR days, while the present-day view shows an aggregates train from Ardingly to Whatley in the hands of Class 66 No 66069. *Lens of Sutton/TG*

REDISCOVERING RAILWAYS

HORLEY (1) had lost its goods yard by 1968, leaving both the signal box and goods shed isolated from the railway they once served. The goods shed was built by the LBSCR as an engine shed.

For once common sense has prevailed and the goods shed has been retained for use as a warehouse for a business concern. The signal box has, however, been demolished. The main line to Brighton is immediately to the left in both photographs.

HORLEY (2) was an imposing station with platforms serving both the Redhill and Quarry Line routes, as seen here during the postwar SR period.

On 26 April 2001 engineering works on the Quarry Line resulted in Gatwick Expresses being routed via Redhill. Newly introduced Class 460 No 460004 works a mid-afternoon train from Victoria to Gatwick Airport. The platforms

GATWICK AIRPORT (1): Past and present on the same day. Almost all the Class 73-hauled 'Gatwick Express' trains had been superceded by Class 460 eight-coach units by the spring of 2002, but on 23 March Class 73 No 73211 was still being used. In the same platform half an hour later is the new order, in the form of the first member of the Class, No 460001.

GATWICK AIRPORT (2): The Brighton line beyond Horley is almost perfectly straight for several miles and one view is very much like any other. Before the construction of the present-day Gatwick Airport station by BR on the site of the long-closed LBSCR Gatwick Racecourse station, this is what the line looked like, except of course that 2-BIL or other SR stock would be working this train, rather than Class 423s seen in 1992.

Gatwick Airport station can be viewed from a nearby public footbridge and in the station on 1 May 1986 is, from left to right, the 'Gatwick Express' and up and down Brighton semi-fast trains.

Although no substantial changes have been made to the station, on 22 March 2002 the only trains in sight are formed of modern rolling-stock. The Gatwick Express is in the hands of a Class 460 EMU, and the Brighton train is Class 319 dual-voltage unit No 319456.

Opposite page GATWICK AIRPORT (OLD): The SR's Gatwick Airport station was about a mile south of the present-day one, and is seen here on 5 September 1955. It closed in 1958, but the site still shows the remnants; in the 1992 view Class 422 No 2257 passes the remains of the platforms on the extreme left and right. The line passes into West Sussex just beyond here.

REDISCOVERING RAILWAYS

TATTENHAM CORNER BRANCH

PURLEY: On 5 July 1964 the Tattenham Corner branch saw a steam-worked special train hauled by Class M7 No 30053, seen here coming off the branch at Purley. This location normally sees a succession of EMUs from both Tattenham Corner and Caterham, such as Class 455 No 5813 on 5 October 1999.

WOODMANSTERNE is seen here shortly after being opened by the SR in 1932. It consists of an island platform of a similar style to other SR stations such as Stoneleigh and North Sheen. A visit in October 1999 found virtually no changes. *Lens of Sutton/TG*

CHIPSTEAD: On a misty morning, probably in the 1930s, we see the magnificent wooden-post lower-quadrant starter at the country end of Chipstead. The 1999 view shows that the signal has gone, but surprisingly the public right of way over the railway has survived. *Lens of Sutton/TG*

REDISCOVERING RAILWAYS

KINGSWOOD is seen first in pre-Grouping days, showing new ballast and a tidy station. Today the station is still well kept and a plaque on the main station building, which is in private use, commemorates the centenary of the Chipstead Valley Railway in November 1997. In the down platform on 4 October 1999 is Class 456 No 456023 forming the 15.12 service from Charing Cross. *Lens of Sutton/TG*

TADWORTH: The Royal Train, returning empty from Tattenham Corner on 3 June 1964, passes through Tadworth behind 'West Country' Class No 34052 *Lord Dowding*. Today's more mundane traffic is exemplified by Class 456 EMU No 456004 forming the 12.39 Tattenham Corner to Charing Cross service on 4 October 1999.

REDISCOVERING RAILWAYS

TATTENHAM CORNER: Class M7 No 30053, recently arrived on a special train from Waterloo, takes water before its return journey on 5 July 1964. On 4 October 1999 Class 456 No 456008 enters the station with the 12.42 service from Charing Cross.

CATERHAM BRANCH

KENLEY: The first photograph is a post-electrification photograph of Kenley, probably taken just after the Second World War. All the main buildings survive today, and on 30 September 1999 Class 455 No 5832 forms the 10.35 London Bridge to Caterham service. *Lens of Sutton/TG*

WHYTELEAFE: This early 1920s view of Whyteleafe is looking toward Purley. The present-day photograph shows that the footbridge has been replaced and re-sited closer to the level crossing, which is behind the camera. Class 455 No 5810 forms the 10.41 Caterham to London Bridge service on 30 September 1999. *Lens of Sutton/TG*

CATERHAM: SER Class F 4-4-0 heads a train of short-wheelbase coaches at Caterham in an undated photograph probably taken in the 1920s; all engines of this class had been withdrawn by 1930, or had been rebuilt as Class F1, the line having been electrified in 1928.

A multi-storey car park has since been built on the site of the goods yard. Class 455 No 5828 forms the 09.26 service to Victoria on 30 September 1999. *Lens of Sutton/TG*

OXTED LINE

SANDERSTEAD: Just north of Sanderstead station, up and down Oxted line trains cross on 5 September 1959. The approaching train is the 11.08am Victoria to Tunbridge Wells West hauled by Class 4MT No 80017, while the up train is the 9.55am Brighton to Victoria hauled by an unidentified 'Mogul'.

The line is now very enclosed, and at the same location, seen through a telephoto lens on 13 October 1999, Class 4VEP (423) No 3535 forms the 13.08 East Grinstead to Victoria service.

WOLDINGHAM: Class U1 No 31899 tackles the climb through Woldingham at the head of the 3.38pm train from Victoria to Brighton and Eastbourne on 5 September 1959.

The platforms have been extended at Woldingham and the same view can be had from the up platform. On 4 April 2002 the 17.10 London Bridge to Uckfield service is worked by Class 205 Nos 205012 (two-coach unit) and 205033 (three-coach unit).

OXTED was an interesting station with steam services from London to various destinations including East Grinstead, Tunbridge Wells, Eastbourne and Brighton. There was also a push-pull service which ran only between Oxted and Tunbridge Wells (or Tonbridge). Bays on both the up and down sides were provided at the south end of the station for these services. On 26 May 1962 Class H No 31005 has just worked the 11.00 from Tunbridge Wells West.

The line from London as far as East Grinstead has been electrified, while the former Brighton line is worked by DMUs as far as Uckfield, but abandoned therefrom. The Eastbourne line is closed, but between Groombridge and Tunbridge Wells West the line forms part of the Spa Valley Railway. Oxted station has been rebuilt and EMUs Nos 3476 and 3095 of Class 423 pass on the Victoria and East Grinstead services in August 1989.

HURST GREEN HALT: A Tunbridge Wells West to Oxted train stops at the station in the spring of 1960. Even as late as this, some of these trains were still formed of pre-Grouping stock.

REDISCOVERING RAILWAYS

The same location from a higher vantage point in 1992 shows that the station has been relocated to the other side of the road bridge; this took place in 1961. The East Grinstead line is on the left and that to Uckfield on the right, which DMU Class 205 No 205024 has just left with the 08.12 Uckfield to Oxted train on 8 August 1989.

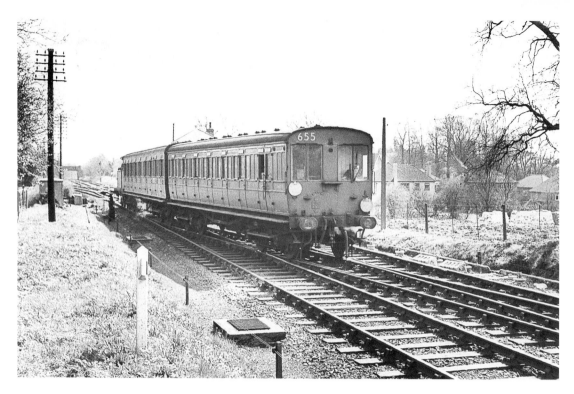

HURST GREEN JUNCTION: Push-pull set No 655, propelled by an 'H' Class engine, negotiates the junction with an Oxted-bound train in April 1960.

The public footpath across the railway has been replaced by a footbridge which gives a slightly different view of the junction. Class 205 No 205023 leads the 07.42 service from Uckfield to London Bridge on 8 August 1989.

LINGFIELD station on a dismal day in 1968. On race days there were additional steam trains from London and hence the need for a more substantial station than the local traffic demanded.

A visit on 10 April 1992 shows few changes other than the loss of the running lines on the right and the second footbridge at the south end of the station, necessitating a platform level photograph. Class 423 No 3442 enters the station forming the 11.10 Victoria to East Grinstead service.

SURREY: THE EAST OF THE COUNTY

DORMANS had through trains to London only during peak hours and this train, hauled by Class '4MT' No 80014 is the 5.25pm East Grinstead to London, photographed in May 1961.

There is currently a half-hourly electric service to London, in this instance formed by Class 4VEP (423) No 3442.

NORTH DOWNS LINE

GODSTONE (1): Looking towards Tonbridge, a Redhill-bound freight train is seen passing Godstone on 8 September 1962 hauled by Class N No 31864.

Class 101 No L588, forming the 10.43 Tonbridge to Reigate service, prepares to pick up passengers in April 1992. The station buildings have been discarded and replaced by rather crude huts, and the third rail is in place pending electrification.

GODSTONE (2) in September 1962 sees Class 4MT No 80015 on the 16.11 Redhill to Tonbridge train. Because of the need for a reversal at Redhill, Reading to Redhill and Redhill to Tonbridge sections of the line were worked independently, often with poor connections at Redhill.

The situation improved with the advent of DMUs, but since electrification through workings from the Reading-Redhill section have ceased. There are, however, freight and engineers' trains using the line, and on 10 April 1992 Class 33 No 33025 *Sultan* takes a ballast train to Tonbridge.

NUTFIELD: The 11.35am Tonbridge to Redhill train leaves Nutfield on 8 September 1962 behind Class 4MT No 80018. A visit 30 years later on 10 April 1992 found that houses were being built on the goods yard site. Class 101 DMU No L594 forms the 09.43 Tonbridge to Redhill service.

SOUTHERN RAILWAY.
NUTFIELD
The holder is prohibited from entering the Company's trains. Not Transferable
Admit ONE to PLATFORM
AVAILABLE ONE HOUR 1 D.
This Ticket must be given up on leaving Platform.
FOR CONDITIONS SEE BACK
1 | 2 | 3 | 4 | 5 | 6
3245

A much more attractive view was obtained from the station itself, where Class 33 No 33025 was seen on an engineers' train on the same day.

REDISCOVERING RAILWAYS

Opposite page REDHILL (1): In September 1962 Class 4MT No 80139 curves away from the station with the 5.11pm train from Redhill to Tonbridge; the station is hidden from view by the goods shed, while the locomotive depot is to the left of the train.

Thirty years later in April 1992 little has changed, other than the growth of the silver birch trees to block the view.

REDHILL (2): In the foreground is the Brighton line, and curving sharply to the west is the Reading line. On 10 April 1992 Class 101 No L836 forms the 09.20 Gatwick Airport to Reading service. A modern DMU in the form of Class 166 No 166208 works the same service on 5 October 1999.

REIGATE on 26 May 1962 is host to the 9.43am Redhill to Guildford train behind Class N No 31821, and EMU Class 2BIL No 2144 on the shuttle service from Redhill.

On 10 April 1992 Class 101 No L841 forms the 08.43 all-stations (except Wanborough) Tonbridge to Reading service.

REDISCOVERING RAILWAYS

BETCHWORTH (1): The 3.04pm Redhill to Reading train is seen near Betchworth on 28 April 1962 behind Class U No 31636.

A public footpath still gives access to this location, and on 27 August 1996 Class 166 No 166206 passes the same point forming the 11.34 Reading to Gatwick Airport service.

REDISCOVERING RAILWAYS

BETCHWORTH (2) is just round the corner beyond the rear of the train in the 'past' photograph taken on 28 April 1962, showing Class N No 31866 working the 10.50am Wolverhampton to Margate train.

The infrastructure train, seen at the same place on 27 August 1996, has only come from Woking, and is hauled by Class 37 No 37106.

BETCHWORTH (3) station is in an attractive location and was adjacent to a quarry with its own railway network with transfer sidings. On 24 April 1962 Class S15 No 30847 trundles through the station with a ballast train to Redhill.

Betchworth has been tastefully maintained complete with 'gas' lamps, apparently a retrograde step as in the 1960s the station was lit by electricity! Class 119 No L594 forms the 07.21 Reading to Tonbridge train on 10 April 1992.

BETCHWORTH (4): On 18 January 1958 Class U No 31798 approaches Betchworth with the 10.39am Reading to Redhill train. I have visited Betchworth on many occasions since then, and the 'present' photograph was taken 38 years later on 27 August 1996. Class 166 No 166221 is forming the 11.34 semi-fast train from Reading to Gatwick Airport. Although the sidings on both sides have gone, the crossover has been retained.

BETCHWORTH (5): On 5 March 1960 the 12.05pm Reading to Redhill train is seen between Betchworth and Deepdene behind an unidentified 'Mogul'. The quarry in the background is hidden by trees in the summer 1996 view, showing a Class 166 on a Gatwick Airport train.

DEEPDENE station is on the embankment that carries the North Downs route over the Leatherhead to Horsham line. On a winter's afternoon in poor light in 1965, Class 4MT No 76059 works a Tonbridge to Reading train.

Deepdene has since lost its original wooden buildings and cast-iron lamp-posts. On 15 March 1992 Class 101 No L838 enters the station with the 09.28 Gatwick Airport to Reading service. Deepdene is now known as Dorking (Deepdene) and, despite being little more than a traditional halt, is now the main station serving Dorking on this line.

DORKING TOWN (1) was a pleasant station where all trains, except some inter-Regional services, stopped. On 28 April 1962 Class U No 31638 heads the 09.03 Reading to Redhill train.

The station has since been renamed Dorking West and now has only a peak-period service. In the early spring of 1996 Class 165 No 165122 passes through the station forming the 11.35 Reading to Redhill service.

DORKING TOWN (2) boasted an impressive building, but even in 1970 it was boarded up and tickets had to be obtained on the train.

The station has suffered what can only be described as official vandalism. Everything has been destroyed and one of the few identifying landmarks is the tall tree in the far left background, still standing after over 20 years. Comparison of the cars on the station forecourt shows that at least one 1960s car has survived man's desire to destroy everything that is old.

GOMSHALL & SHERE (1): An ex-GWR engine, Class 4300 No 6379, enters the station with a BR Mark I set forming the 11.05 Redhill to Guildford train on 28 April 1962. The platforms are staggered; that for Guildford trains is behind the camera.

Apart from the signal box, all buildings have been replaced and the station name reduced to Gomshall. The service has also been reduced and trains only stop here at peak times on weekdays. On 23 October 1992 Class 47 No 47847 passes through with the 14.20 Brighton to Manchester train.

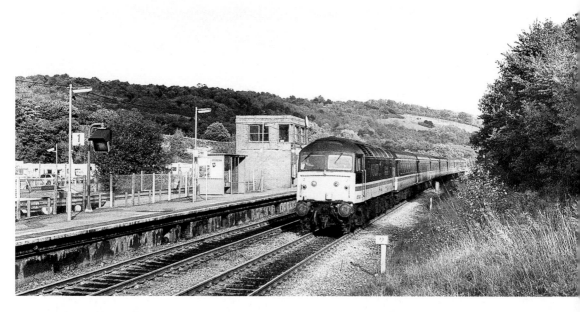

Opposite page GOMSHALL & SHERE (2): A heavy freight train climbs into Gomshall & Shere station on 28 April 1962 behind Class N No 31842. At the same location on 17 October 1996 a lightweight infrastructure train is hauled by Class 37 No 37242.

REDISCOVERING RAILWAYS

ALBURY BANK: A Redhill to Reading train is seen on Albury Bank hauled by Class N No 31862 in February 1965. A more elevated view at the same location on 4 April 1997 shows a Class 37 hauling two Class 73s towards Redhill.

REDISCOVERING RAILWAYS

CHILWORTH & ALBURY (1): Class 4MT No 80017 has just left Chilworth & Albury with the 1.50pm Reading to Redhill train. In the second view, dated 5 November 1996, the station is just visible in the background as preserved Class S15 No 828 in SR livery takes a special train towards Redhill.

CHILWORTH & ALBURY (2): Class U No 31638 is seen at the station on 28 April 1962. The small waiting shelter on the right is typical of those found throughout the former SECR system and indeed on many stations rebuilt by the SR.

Today the shelter and lamp hut at the end of the platform have both gone, and the footbridge, from which the 'past' photograph was taken, has also been removed, necessitating a platform-level photograph. On 1 October 1996 Class 166 No 166207 speeds through Chilworth with the 14.03 Gatwick Airport to Reading service.

SHALFORD (1): The odd combination of a GWR locomotive on a former SECR line in Surrey. Class 4300 No 5385 passes Shalford on the 09.02 Margate to Birmingham service on 27 August 1960. Through services from Kent have long since ceased to operate.

On 20 March 1997 Class 165 No 165003 negotiates the crossover at the east end of the station, having arrived as the 11.07 service from Reading, which terminates here; it will return to Reading at 12.09. The reason for providing Shalford with this service is more to do with avoiding berthing charges at Guildford than customer demand.

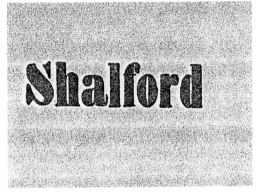

SHALFORD (2): Ex-GWR engines were frequently seen on the Reading to Redhill trains on summer Saturdays when they worked both the local services and through trains from other Regions. Class 4300 No 6387 leaves Shalford with a rake of Maunsell coaches forming the 11.05 Redhill to Guildford service on 27 August 1960. Through services were later discontinued, but from 1992 some trains from Brighton to the North of England were rerouted over the North Downs line.

On 15 May 1992 Class 101 No L839 has just left the station with the 15.26 Gatwick Airport to Reading service.

REDISCOVERING RAILWAYS

SHALFORD BRIDGE: The railway crosses the River Wey on a girder bridge just before the junction with the Portsmouth main line, which is visible in the background as Class N No 31824 takes the 2.50pm Reading to Redhill train over the bridge.

A short infrastructure train hauled by Class 37 No 37137 has just crossed the bridge (beyond the signal) on 20 March 1997.

GAZETTEER OF EAST SURREY'S RAILWAYS

Mileages are taken from the Southern Region Passenger Services Timetable, 12 September 1960, where possible. Stations were opened and closed on the same dates as their respective lines, unless otherwise quoted.

Suburban lines

Wimbledon to West Croydon (joint LSWR/LBSCR to Merton Park, then LBSCR)

Stations in Surrey (1960s boundary): Mitcham (2½m), Mitcham Junction (3m), Beddington Lane Halt (3¾m), Waddon Marsh Halt (5m) and West Croydon (6¼m). The new tramway stations over this section are Belgrave Walk, Mitcham, Mitcham Junction, Beddington Lane, Therapia Lane, Ampere Way, Waddon Marsh, Wandle Park, Reeves Corner and West Croydon.

Beddington Lane Halt was called Beddington until 1.1887 and West Croydon was Croydon Town until 4.1851. West Croydon was rebuilt in 1933/34.

Opening and closure: Line opened 22.10.1855 and electrified 6.7.1930. Mitcham Junction opened 1.10.1868, Waddon Marsh Halt opened 6.7.1930 and West Croydon 5.6.1839. Line closed 5.1997 (except Mitcham Junction and West Croydon stations); due to re-open as a tramway 4.11.1999, but delayed until 30.5.2000.

Route and traffic: A single line for passenger trains (from Merton Park) passing through residential and industrial areas, as well as the large open space of Mitcham Common. At Mitcham Junction it was dissected by the Victoria and London Bridge to Sutton line. From Wandle Park it ran parallel to the Sutton to West Croydon line and had its own bay at West Croydon. Passenger numbers have always been light, and after electrification trains were normally formed of two coaches only. There was a separate freight-only line from West Croydon to Beddington Lane. There was much traffic on this section, primarily to serve a power station and gas works at Waddon Marsh.

Wimbledon to Sutton via South Merton (SR)

Stations in Surrey: Morden South (2m) , St Helier (2½m), Sutton Common (3½m), West Sutton (4¼m), Sutton (5¼m).

Opening: Wimbledon to South Merton opened 7.7.1929 and South Merton to Sutton 5.1.1930. Sutton opened 10.5.1847. Line electrified from the outset.

Route and traffic: The line has sharp curves and severe gradients most of the way. It was built to serve new housing estates. The only goods facilities were at Morden South where there was a rail link to a milk depot with at least one train of tankers per day. The area surrounding the line has become increasingly populated and its only function is the conveyance of local passengers. The milk depot no longer has rail access.

Mitcham Junction to Sutton (LBSCR)

Stations: Mitcham Junction (0m), Hackbridge (1m), Carshalton (2m), Sutton (3¼m).

Opening: Line opened 1.10.1868. Sutton opened 10.5.1847. Line electrified 3.3.1929.

Route and traffic: The line leaves Mitcham Junction on a sharp curve and skirts Mitcham Common before reaching a residential area that starts at Hackbridge. There was little goods traffic and the line is now exclusively passenger, including both local and Thameslink services.

West Croydon to Leatherhead and Horsham (LBSCR, joint with LSWR between Epsom and Leatherhead)

Stations: West Croydon (0m), Waddon (1¼m), Bandon Halt (2m), Wallington (2¾m), Carshalton Beeches (3½m), Sutton (4½m), Cheam (5½m), Ewell East (7m), Epsom Town (8m), Epsom (8½m), Ashtead (10½m), Leatherhead (12¼m), Boxhill (15½m), Dorking North (16¼m), Holmwood (21¼m), Ockley & Capel (23½m); remaining stations in West Sussex.

West Croydon was called Croydon Town until 4.1851. Wallington was known as Carshalton until 1.9.1868. Carshalton Beeches opened as Beeches Halt and was renamed 1.4.1925. Epsom Town was also known as Epsom until 9.7.1923. A new station was built at Epsom in 1929. Ewell East was Ewell until 9.7.1923. Boxhill was called West Humble until 1.11.1870, then Box Hill & Burford Bridge until 5.1896, Box Hill until 12.1904, then Box Hill & Burford Bridge again until the 1960s, when it became to Boxhill & Westhumble. Dorking North was Dorking until 9.7.1923 and again from 11.5.1987. Ockley & Capel was Ockley until 1.7.1869, Ockley & Capel until 1.4.1887, then Ockley again until it changed back to Ockley & Capel 15.9.1952; it is currently called Ockley for the third time.

Opening and closure: Line opened from West Croydon to Epsom Town 10.5.1847, and from Epsom Town to Epsom 8.8.1859. Epsom to Leatherhead opened 1.2.1859, Leatherhead to Dorking 11.3.1867, and Dorking to Horsham 1.5.1867. A spur connecting Dorking LBSCR to the SER line opened on 1.5.1867; relegated to use as a carriage siding between 1900 and 1926, it was reconnected 3.9.1941 and removed 1947.

West Croydon opened 5.6.1839. Waddon opened 2.1863. Bandon Halt opened 11.6.1906 and closed 7.6.1914. A new station was built at Wallington 9.1883 and again 1983. Carshalton Beeches opened 1.10.1906. Epsom Town closed to passengers 3.3.1929 and to goods 3.5.1965. Leatherhead (joint LSWR/LBSCR) opened 1.2.1859 and closed 4.3.1867, when separate LSWR and LBSCR stations were opened. LSWR station closed 10.7.1927.

West Croydon to Sutton electrified 1.4.1925, Raynes Park to Dorking North 12.7.1925. London Bridge to Mitcham Junction, Dorking North and Effingham Junction, also Victoria to Epsom, all electrified 3.3.1929. Victoria to Sutton electrified (overhead system) 1.4.1925 and converted to third rail 22.9.1929.

Route and traffic: Between West Croydon and Epsom the line is undulating with a maximum gradient of 1 in 90 between West Croydon and Waddon. At Leatherhead the line picks up the River Mole, passing through the Mole Gap in a short tunnel. On leaving Dorking North the line passes under the Redhill to Guildford line, then enters another tunnel. Curves are more frequent on the section from here to the border with West Sussex, with long stretches on embankment. The line has always been predominantly for passenger trains, although there were regular freight trains between West Croydon and Epsom Town. There is currently a very frequent passenger service as far as Epsom. Between Epsom and Leatherhead trains also come from Waterloo via Wimbledon and only these continue to Dorking. Stations beyond Dorking are served by an hourly train from Victoria via Sutton. There is no Sunday service on this section.

Epsom Downs branch (LBSCR)

Stations: Sutton (0m), Belmont (1¼m), Banstead (2¾m), Epsom Downs (4¼m).

Belmont was named California until 1.10.1875, and Banstead was Banstead & Burgh Heath between 1.6.1898 and 8.1928.

Opening: Line opened 22.5.1865 and electrified (from London Bridge) 17.6.1928. Goods facilities were withdrawn 6.1.1969. Line singled 3.10.1982. Epsom Downs re-sited ¼ mile towards Sutton 14.2.1989.

Route and traffic: The line leaves Sutton on a sharp curve and climbs at a maximum of 1 in 58 to Banstead after which there is a slight fall followed by a rise on the approach to Epsom Downs. It traverses Banstead Downs in a deep cutting. The line was built for race traffic and for local patronage from the intermediate stations. Goods were a secondary consideration. Railmotors were mainly used until electrification, which provided a half-hour-interval service for many years. The line has never been as heavily used by commuters as many of the other suburban lines. Extra trains have always been provided on race days and occasionally the Royal Train has taken this route. Outside peak periods the service is currently hourly, with no service on Sundays.

Brighton main line and branches

Brighton main line (LBSCR and SER)

Stations in Surrey: East Croydon (0m), South Croydon (1m) , Purley Oaks (2¼m), Purley (3m), Stoats Nest (4¼m), Coulsdon North (4¾m, LBSCR), Coulsdon South (4¾m, SER), Merstham (8½m), Redhill (10½m), Earlswood (11¼m, LBSCR), Salfords (13¼m, LBSCR), Horley (15½m, LBSCR), Gatwick Racecourse (16¼m, LBSCR), Gatwick Airport (16¼, BR), Gatwick Airport (17m, LBSCR).

For Purley, see Tattenham Corner branch entry below. Coulsdon North was Stoats Nest until 1.6.1911, Coulsdon & Smitham Downs until 9.7.1923 and Coulsdon West until 1.8.1923. Coulsdon South was Coulsdon until 3.1896, Coulsdon & Cane Hill until 9.7.1923 and Coulsdon East until 1.8.1923. Redhill was named Reigate until 4.7.1849, Reigate Junction until 8.1858 and Redhill Junction until 7.1929. Gatwick Airport was Tinsley Green (for Gatwick Airport) until 1.6.1936.

Opening and closure: Croydon Junction (Norwood) to Haywards Heath opened 12.7.1841. SER had running powers over LBSCR line as far as Reigate Junction (Redhill) until 19.7.1842, when line was purchased by SER beginning just north of present-day Coulsdon South to Redhill. South Croydon to Stoats Nest (second station) opened 5.11.1899, Stoats Nest to Earlswood for freight also 5.11.1899, but not for passengers until 1.4.1900.

Balham to Coulsdon North electrified (overhead) 1.4.1925 and converted to third rail 22.9.1929. Purley to Three Bridges electrified 17.7.1932.

Purley Oaks opened 5.11.1899. Stoats Nest closed 1.12.1856, replaced by new station of same name 5.11.1899, which closed (as Coulsdon North) 1.10.1983. Coulsdon South opened (as Coulsdon) 1.10.1889. Merstham opened 1.12.1841 and closed 1.10.1843; re-sited station ½ mile north opened by SER 4.10.1844. Redhill had LBSCR and SER stations, both known as Reigate, which closed 5.1844. Redhill (still known as Reigate) (SER) opened 5.1844 on site of present station, rebuilt 1858. Salfords opened as a halt 8.10.1915, replaced by another halt of same name 17.7.1932, and became a station 1.1.1935. Gatwick Racecourse opened 1891. Gatwick Airport closed 28.5.1958 and station of same name opened on site of Gatwick Racecourse station 27.5.1958.

New line (Quarry Line) built by LBSCR from Coulsdon North to Earlswood (6½m) bypassing Merstham and Redhill, with no intermediate stations. Opened for freight 8.11.1899 and passengers 1.4.1900.

Route and traffic: The main line runs north-south in a valley with no significant curves, climbing gently towards the North Downs. It passes through a tunnel at Merstham Gap, then descends gradually to Redhill. From Horley it climbs gently to the county boundary and beyond. The Quarry Line crosses over the original line 1¾ miles south of Coulsdon North, running parallel on its eastern side through its own tunnel at Merstham Gap. It bypasses Redhill through a tunnel that also takes it under the Tonbridge to Redhill line. It joins the original line just beyond this point. Traffic has always been predominantly passenger, both local and long distance between London and Brighton. The line also saw trains from other parts of the country, and this continues to the present day. There were both local and long-distance freight trains, and although general freight has ceased there are stone depots at Purley and Salfords (and Ardingly), all of which have regular trains.

Tattenham Corner branch (SER)

Stations: Purley (0m), Reedham (¾m), Smitham (1½m), Woodmansterne (2¼m), Chipstead (3¼m), Kingswood (5¾m), Tadworth (7m), Tattenham Corner (8¼m).

Reedham was a halt until 5.7.1936. Chipstead

was named Chipstead & Banstead Downs until 9.7.1923. Kingswood was Kingswood & Burgh Heath until 1968. Tadworth was Tadworth & Walton on the Hill until 1.7.1900. *Opening and closure:* Purley to Kingswood opened 2.11.1897, Kingswood to Tadworth 1.7.1900 and Tadworth to Tattenham Corner 4.6.1901. Line electrified from Charing Cross to Tadworth 25.3.1928 and to Tattenham Corner 17.6.1928.

Purley opened as Godstone Road 12.4.1841, closed 1.10.1847, re-opened as Caterham Junction 5.8.1856, and renamed Purley 1.10.1888. Reedham opened 1.3.1911 and Smitham 1.1.1904, but both closed between 1.1.1917 and 1.1.1919. Woodmansterne opened 17.7.1932. From 1907 Tattenham Corner was little used other than by race trains. It was closed to regular services between 9.1914 and 25.3.1928, but was used by military trains and, after the war, also by race trains. Regular passenger services were re-instated from 25.3.1928.

Route and traffic: The line leaves Purley on the east side of the Brighton main line and after the Caterham branch diverges, it passes under the main line to run parallel with it on the west side as far as Smitham. The line runs in the Chipstead Valley and climbs all the way from Reedham almost to Tadworth at a maximum of 1 in 75, and thereafter falls to Tattenham Corner. There are two short tunnels between Kingswood and Tadworth. The line was built mainly for passenger traffic and particularly for Epsom races. It still serves these functions and the Royal Train normally uses this line for Derby Day. For the remainder of the year the line is well used by commuters. Freight ceased in May 1962. There is currently a half-hourly service on weekdays, with extra trains at peak periods. On Sundays an hourly service is provided. There are additional trains that terminate at Smitham, these being introduced following the closure of Coulsdon North, which was adjacent.

Caterham branch (SER)

Stations: Purley (0m), Kenley (1¼m), Whyteleafe (2½m), Whyteleafe South (3m), Caterham (4¾m).

Kenley was known as Coulsdon until 12.1856. Whyteleafe South opened as Marden Road, renamed Warlingham 1.1.1894 and took its present name 11.6.1956.

Opening: Line opened 5.8.1856 as Caterham Railway and became part of SER in 1859. Electrified 25.3.1928. Whyteleafe opened 1.1.1900 and replaced private Halliloo Platform, which was situated a little to the south.

Route and traffic: The line was built along the Caterham Valley, mainly for passenger traffic. There were also occasional troop trains. It climbs at a maximum of 1 in 90 all the way to the terminus. A frequent service has been provided for decades to cater for the rapid growth in the number of commuters. The present-day service consists of four trains an hour in each direction throughout the day, with an hourly service on Sundays. Freight was light and ceased in September 1964.

Oxted line (SER and LBSCR)

Stations in Surrey: East Croydon (0m), South Croydon (1m), Selsdon (1¼m), Sanderstead (2m), Purley Downs Golf Course Halt, Riddlesdown (3¼m), Upper Warlingham (5m), Woldingham (6¾m), Oxted (10m), Hurst Green Halt (11m), Crowhurst Junction North (no station, 13¼m), Lingfield (16m), Dormans (17½m); Hurst Green Halt (11m), Monks Lane Halt (13¼m); remainder of lines are in West Sussex.

East Croydon known as East Croydon Main, and East Croydon Local until 7.1924. East Croydon Local called New Croydon until 1.6.1909. Woldingham called Marden Park until 1.1.1894. Upper Warlingham called Upper Warlingham & Whyteleafe between 1.1.1894 and 1.10.1900. Oxted called Oxted & Limpsfield until 1969.

Opening and closure: East Croydon opened 12.7.1841. More platforms added 1860 by LBSCR and given name New Croydon. Station rebuilt 1898 and again 1991/92. South Croydon opened 1.9.1865. South Croydon to East Grinstead opened 10.3.1884 (SER/LBSCR joint to Crowhurst Junction, then LBSCR). Selsdon Road opened 1885, but little used between 1.1.1917 and 30.9.1935, when it re-opened as Selsdon; closed to Oxted line trains 15.6.1959. Purley Downs Golf Course Halt opened about 1914 and closed 1927. Riddlesdown opened 5.6.1927. Woldingham opened 1.7.1885 as Marden Park. Hurst Green Halt opened 1.6.1907, re-sited 12.6.1961 and suffix 'Halt' dropped. Crowhurst Junction North to Crowhurst Junction South (on Tonbridge to Redhill line) closed 13.6.1955. Monks Lane Halt opened 1.6.1907 and closed 11.9.1939. South Croydon to Oxted and East Grinstead electrified 10.1987.

Route and traffic: The line climbs at 1 in 83 from the junction with the main line to Selsdon, beyond which the gradient is 1 in 100 most of the way to the summit just beyond Woldingham. After Riddlesdown the line enters a tunnel, then crosses a viaduct before reaching Upper Warlingham. The descent starts more gradually and the line passes through Oxted Tunnel; after Oxted station it is carried on a viaduct, then through a short tunnel before reaching Hurst Green, the junction for the East Grinstead and Tunbridge Wells lines. The former line continues to fall most of the way to the county boundary. The line was, and still is, predominantly for passenger traffic, and normal services were augmented on race days at Lingfield. There was considerable locally generated goods in the early years (lime, bricks, livestock), but this ceased completely in the 1960s. The present weekday service consists of half-hourly trains from Victoria to East Grinstead, with an hourly connecting train at Oxted for Uckfield. There are additional trains at peak periods.

Woodside to Addiscombe (SER) and Woodside to Selsdon Junction and Sanderstead (joint SER/LBSCR)

Stations: Woodside (0m), Addiscombe (1m); Woodside (0m), Bingham Road (¾m), Coombe Road (1¾m), Spencer Road Halt (2m), Selsdon (2¼m).

Woodside was renamed Woodside & South Norwood 1.10.1908, and Woodside (Surrey) 2.10.1944. Addiscombe was named Croydon (Addiscombe Road) until 1.4.1925 when it became Croydon (Addiscombe). It was renamed Addiscombe 3.1926, but from 1935 at the latest until the 1950s was shown in public timetables as Addiscombe (Croydon). Coombe Road was named Coombe Lane until 30.9.1935.

Opening and closure: Woodside to Addiscombe opened 1.4.1864, and electrified 28.2.1926. Branch closed May 1997 and has been converted into a tramway, which opened 23.5.2000 as part of a new line between Croydon and Beckenham. Woodside to Selsdon opened 10.8.1885, closed (other than to a few Oxted line trains) 1.1.1917 and re-opened 30.9.1935. Woodside to Sanderstead electrified 30.9.1935, when Selsdon Road was renamed Selsdon. Bingham Road opened 1.9.1906, closed 15.3.1915, and re-opened 30.9.1935. Coombe Road opened 10.8.1885, closed 1.1.1917, and re-opened 30.9.1935. All three stations closed with the line 13.5.1983. Spencer Road Halt opened 1.9.1906 and closed 15.3.1915.

Route and traffic: Both lines from Woodside were built for local traffic, although surprisingly neither developed as many other electrified suburban lines. In the 1950s both lines had two trains per hour on weekdays (with extras at peak periods). The Sanderstead service was later reduced to peak hours only until closure of the line. Addiscombe is no longer a terminus, as following re-opening trams run between Beckenham Junction and Croydon at 10-minute intervals.

North Downs line (SER)

Stations in Surrey: From Tonbridge (0m) stations are in Kent until Godstone (14m), Nutfield (17½m), Redhill (19½m), Reigate (1¾m from Redhill), Betchworth (4½m), Deepdene (7¼m), Dorking Town (8m), Westcott Range Halt (9½m), Gomshall & Shere (12¾m), Chilworth & Albury (16¾m), Shalford (18½m), then to Guildford and Reading.

Reigate was called Reigate Town until 1.11.1898. Deepdene was Box Hill & Leatherhead Road until 3.1851, then Box Hill until 9.7.1923, and changed to Dorking (Deepdene) 11.5.1987. Dorking Town was called Dorking until 9.7.1923, and changed to Dorking West 11.5.1987. Gomshall & Shere was renamed Gomshall, and Chilworth & Albury was renamed Chilworth, in the early 1980s.

Opening and closure: Reigate Junction to Tonbridge opened 26.5.1842, and Nutfield opened 1883. Reigate Junction to Dorking opened 4.7.1849. Dorking to Shalford opened 20.8.1849 and Shalford to Guildford 15.10.1849, with running powers over the LSWR from Shalford Junction. Dorking spur connecting this line with Leatherhead to Horsham line opened 1.5.1867, closed 1900, re-instated 3.9.1941, but dismantled 1947. Westcott Range Halt opened 11.1916 and closed about 1928. Redhill to Reigate electrified 17.7.1932, and Redhill to Tonbridge 1994.

Route and traffic: The line runs in a westerly direction all the way from Tonbridge and is almost perfectly straight to the outskirts of Redhill. On entering Surrey it passes over the Oxted to East Grinstead line. Between Godstone and Nutfield is Bletchingley Tunnel. The line descends from Nutfield and approaches Redhill from the south on a sharp curve.

The line to Guildford turns sharply west at the south end of Redhill and is crossed by several road overbridges in the densely populated section to Reigate. Beyond Reigate the land is sparsely populated with only villages, farmhouses and the open country of the Surrey Hills. At Betchworth there was a transfer siding for the lime works' narrow gauge system. On the outskirts of Dorking the line crosses the Leatherhead to Horsham line. It begins its climb in earnest on leaving Dorking as it continues along the south edge of the Surrey Hills for 4 miles at a maximum of 1 in 96. It then descends at the same gradient through Gomshall, after which there is a short climb, before continuing to descend almost to Shalford.

For most of their existence the lines east and west of Redhill were operated independently. More recently there has been integration of services, but through trains no longer run between Guildford and Tonbridge. Since electrification of the eastern section there have been fast trains from Tonbridge to Redhill and Gatwick Airport; some all-stations trains continue to London. On the western section there are fast trains between Redhill, Guildford and Reading; intermediate stations are served bi-hourly. Also in recent years a direct service between Gatwick Airport and Reading has been operating. Even in SER days there were through trains from the North West of England and from the GWR to the Kent Coast, with a reversal at Redhill, and this practice continues to the present day, with some Virgin Trains to Brighton running via Guildford. Both sections of the line have always seen heavy freight traffic, nowadays mainly infrastructure trains.

INDEX OF LOCATIONS

Page numbers in **bold** refer to the photographs; other entries refer to the Gazetteer section.